GREAT ⊕ CIVILISATIONS

ANCIENT EGYPT

Anita Ganeri

FRANKLIN WATTS
LONDON•SYDNEY

First published in 2014 by Franklin Watts

Copyright © Franklin Watts 2014

Franklin Watts
338 Euston Road
London NW1 3BH

Franklin Watts Australia
Level 17/207 Kent Street
Sydney, NSW 2000

A CIP catalogue record for the book is available from the British Library.

Dewey number: 932

Hardback ISBN 978 1 4451 3329 4
Library eBook ISBN 978 1 4451 3330 0

Printed in China

Franklin Watts is a division of Hachette Children's Books,
an Hachette UK company.

www.hachette.co.uk

Editor: Sarah Ridley
Editor in Chief: John C. Miles
Series designer: John Christopher/White Design
Art director: Peter Scoulding
Picture research: Diana Morris

Picture credits
The Art Archive/Alamy: 19, 25t. The Art Gallery Collection/Alamy: 29. Bakha/CC
Wikipedia: 11. BM pix /istockphoto: 22. Judy Ditton/istockphoto: 5. Donyanedomam/
istockphoto: 26. Tor Eigeland/Alamy: 13. Francis Xavier Espuny/Dreamstime: 20-21.
Werner Forman /Alamy: 9. Werner Forman/Getty Images: 6, 12. Robert Harding/Corbis:
8. Jim Henderson/Alamy: 27. Iberfoto/Superstock: 16, 18. Michael Janosek/Dreamstime:
24-25. Doctor Jools/istockphoto: 14. Terry J Lawrence/istockphoto: 17. Amanda Lewis/
istockphoto: 7. mareandmare/Shutterstock: front cover, 1. McSavva/istockphoto: 28.
Science & Society PL/Superstock: 10. Jose Ignacio Soto/istockphoto: 4.
Superstock: 20. UIG/Getty Images: 23. Berthold Werner/CC Wikipedia: 15.

CONTENTS

ANCIENT EGYPT

The ancient Egyptians lived from around 3000–30 BCE and built up one of the greatest and longest-lasting civilisations in the world. Their brilliant achievements still survive today in the many buildings and objects that they left behind. These have helped archaeologists to piece together a fascinating picture of what Egyptian life was like.

4

Land of the Nile

Ancient Egypt was a long, narrow country, stretching along the River Nile. On either side lay hot, dry desert. The Egyptians called the desert 'Red Land', and considered it a dangerous place. Most people lived in the river valley where, each year, the river flooded, dumping rich, black soil onto the land. This was ideal for farming, the reason behind Egypt's success and wealth.

Cutting edge

We know a great deal about the ancient Egyptians from buildings, paintings, jewellery and many other objects buried in tombs. We also have accounts from ancient writers, such as the Greek historian, Herodotus (c.484–420 BCE). He made a grand tour of ancient Egypt and described many aspects of the culture, including mummification.

One of the most famous pharaohs of ancient Egypt, Ramesses II (1289-1224 BCE) had many statues of himself made (left).

The River Nile in Egypt. Today, most Egyptians still live along the river banks, as they did thousands of years ago.

Kingdoms and pharaohs

Early on, there were two kingdoms in Egypt – Upper Egypt and Lower Egypt. The two were united by King Menes in around 3100 BCE. Ancient Egypt was ruled by a king, called a pharaoh, who was believed to be descended from the sun god. The title 'pharaoh' comes from the Egyptian words *per-o* which mean 'great house'. The pharaoh was so important people felt it was rude to refer to him directly and so titles like this were used instead.

 ## Around the world

c.4000–2000 BCE Sumeria
One of the earliest civilisations grows up in Sumer (modern-day Iraq) on the fertile land around the great Tigris and Euphrates rivers.

. . . .

c.3000–1500 BCE Pakistan/India
The Indus Valley civilisation reaches its peak in around 2500 BCE, with well established cities, including Mohenjo-Daro, and trade routes.

. . . .

c.1600–1460 BCE China
The Shang Dynasty rules in the Yellow River valley region of China. Their capital moves several times, settling in a place, called Anyang.

. . . .

WEAVER'S WORKSHOP

From the earliest times, the ancient Egyptians made their clothes from linen, woven on wooden looms. Weaving was a highly valued skill, and the best weavers were well paid. This model of a weaver's workshop was found in a tomb at Deir el-Bahari.

6

This model of a weaver's workshop was made in c.2000 BCE. It was placed in a tomb to provide the dead person with linen to wear in the next world (see pages 24-25).

Cutting edge

The first Egyptian looms were laid out horizontally, with the warp (lengthwise) threads stretched around two wooden beams. The beams were attached to four short pegs which were pushed into the ground. From around 1500 BCE, vertical looms came into use. These were more practical and took up less space.

From plant to cloth

Linen was made from the stems of the flax plant which grew along the River Nile. Turning it into cloth was a long and complicated process. After harvesting the flax, the stems were soaked and beaten to separate the fibres. The fibres were spun into yarn, then woven into cloth on a loom. In the tomb model (above), some women are spinning yarn, while others are weaving cloth on horizontal looms.

Fabrics and finery

We know what the ancient Egyptians wore from tomb paintings. Men wore short linen loincloths or kilts, tied at the waist. Women wore simple, long dresses. Clothes were usually white. The quality of linen depended on how rich or important the wearer was. A pharaoh wore extremely soft linen, but most people had much rougher cloth.

Ancient Egyptian women wore long, flowing linen dresses, sometimes decorated with sharp, crisp pleats. They wore their hair long, with elaborate plaits and curls.

Around the world

c.5000 BCE Egypt

One of the earliest examples of woven cloth comes from the city of Fayum in Egypt. Strips of linen have also been found in tombs, where they were used to wrap mummies.

c.3000 BCE Pakistan/India

There is a well-developed cotton industry in the Indus Valley. Fragments of cotton cloth have survived, making them some of the earliest traces of cotton in existence.

c.1600–1460 BCE China

Silk is first produced in China in around 2700 BCE but is kept a closely-guarded secret. Fragments of silk cloth have been found in royal tombs from the Shang Dynasty.

LOOKING BEAUTIFUL

Almost everyone in ancient Egypt wore jewellery. Poor people had simple pieces made from copper or faience. For the rich, there were elaborate pieces made from gold, inlaid with semi-precious stones. Amulets were a form of jewellery worn to protect people from harm.

Cutting edge

Egyptian jewellers had fabulous materials to work with. Semi-precious stones, such as carnelian and feldspar, came from the desert; lapis lazuli came from Afghanistan. Gold was beaten into shape or made into objects in moulds. Jewellers also used a technique, called granulation, to create delicate patterns from tiny granules of gold.

8

Made about 1337 BCE, this exquisite scarab pectoral is from Tutankhamun's tomb.

Scarab pectoral

The materials, colours and designs had special meanings. This pectoral (pendant) was found in King Tutankhamun's tomb. It is made from gold, a sacred metal linked to the sun god, Ra. In the centre is a scarab beetle, also representing the sun god. Above it is a boat, carrying an eye – the symbol of the moon. The whole piece is inlaid with stones, such as blue lapis lazuli, which symbolised the heavens.

These pots and
jars once held
cosmetics and perfumes.
They were kept in a small
wooden chest. Many cosmetic
holders have survived, showing
how important appearance was.

Beauty treatments

The ancient Egyptians went to great lengths to look
beautiful. Both men and women wore black eyepaint
to make their eyes look bigger. The paint was made
from ground-up minerals. Lips and cheeks were
painted red with powdered ochre. People stored
their cosmetics in jars and containers, often carved
in the shape of animals.

Around the world

c.2600–2000 BCE Sumeria
Huge quantities of gold and
silver jewellery are buried
in the Royal Tombs of Ur,
including a headdress of gold
leaves and gold ribbons,
worn by Queen Puabi.

c.1900–1000 BCE Pakistan
Highly skilled beadmakers
in Harappa make beads
from semi-precious stones.
Some beads are heated
to produce a prized
red colour.

c.2000 BCE–900 Central America
The Maya make exquisite
jewellery from jade, including
earplugs, worn by the men.
Jade is also traded. It is used
by healers to cure the sick.

TIME AND MEASURING

The ancient Egyptians were expert mathematicians, with advanced systems of numbers and measures. They used their knowledge in many practical ways. Among their inventions were the earliest clocks, units of measurement, and the first calendar to divide the year into 365 days.

Water clocks became the standard way of telling the time in the ancient world. This Egyptian example was made c.1400 BCE.

10

Telling the time

The Egyptians introduced a 24-hour day, divided into 12 hours of day and 12 of night. They used shadow clocks to measure daylight hours. The time was shown by a shadow falling across a marked-out scale. From around 1500 BCE, water clocks were used to tell the time at night. This is the oldest water clock known. It is made from stone with sloping sides and a small hole at the bottom. The bowl of the clock is filled with water, which slowly drips out. A scale of 12 rings, each representing an hour, is carved on the inside to mark the time as the level falls.

Cutting edge

Egyptian astronomers used the Sun, Moon and stars to work out the world's earliest 365-day calendar, around 5,000 years ago. It was used to calculate the date of the annual flooding of the Nile – a vitally important event for Egyptian farmers. The year was divided into 12 months, each 30 days long, with five extra days at the end.

This picture shows a modern reproduction of the Royal Cubit of c.1340 BCE.

Body measures

To measure out their fields, the Egyptians invented a unit of measurement, called the cubit. This was based on the length of a man's arm, from his elbow to his middle fingertip. To avoid confusion, all cubit sticks were measured against the Royal Cubit, a black granite rod about 52 cm long.

11

Around the world

c.2700–2300 BCE Sumeria
The Sumerians invent the abacus, a type of counting frame for adding and subtracting. It uses the Sumerian number system which has a unit of 60 as its base, rather than 10.

c.2000 BCE–900 CE Central America
Two very accurate calendars are used by the Maya – an everyday calendar with 18 months of 20 days plus five odd days, and a sacred 260-day calendar for religious festivals.

c.1600–1460 BCE China
Evidence suggests that outflow water clocks, where the water flows out, may be in use in China. By 200 BCE, they are replaced by inflow water clocks, where the container fills up with water as time passes.

A REVOLUTION IN FARMING

The ancient Egyptians invented ingenious ways to harness the power of the River Nile. One such invention was the shaduf, an irrigation tool that helped farmers to water their crops. The shaduf made it possible for people to live and form year-round communities in the Nile Valley.

12

Nilometers, such as this one at Elephantine, were gauges used to check the depth of the River Nile. Marks on rocks showed the level of floods.

Cutting edge

The ancient Egyptians developed other farming technologies to feed the country's large population. As well as simple tools such as flint-blade sickles, winnowing scoops, hoes and ploughs that turned the soil, they built mud-brick reservoirs to trap the Nile flood waters. During the dry season, the reservoir waters could then be released into a network of irrigation canals dug through the fields.

Harnessing the floods

The River Nile was extremely important to the ancient Egyptians. Without it, this advanced civilisation could not have developed. Stretching down the middle of the country, the Nile is the only source of water in this dry, desert land. Regular flooding of the river began in June each year, irrigating the land around the river with water and mineral-rich silt, perfect for farming.

Water weight

Outside the flooding season, the shaduf made it possible for farmers to keep watering their crops. The shaduf is a simple device made up of a pole balanced on a crossbeam. On one end is a rope and bucket; on the other a heavy counterweight. Farmers worked it by pulling on the rope to lower the bucket into the water, letting the counterweight help them raise the full bucket, and swinging it round to empty water into a ditch leading to their fields.

13

The shaduf is still used by farmers along the Nile today. Its simple design has not changed for thousands of years.

Around the world

2650 BCE Ancient Egypt
Workers begin building a huge dam at Sadd-el-Kafara to control the Nile's floodwaters. The dam is never completed and is itself destroyed by a flood ten years later.

c.1500 BCE Pakistan/India
Most cities of the Indus Valley civilisation are abandoned as the River Indus changes its course and leaves them without water, destroying agriculture and trade.

c.300 BCE China
People living along the Min river experience disastrous yearly floods. Local governor Li Bing orders the building of a huge dyke, redirecting the river so its floodwaters miss towns and cities.

SHIPS AND SAILS

The River Nile was also the main transport route in ancient Egypt. Boats packed the river, carrying passengers and cargo, including massive stones for building. The earliest Egyptian boats were made from papyrus reeds, and were used for short trips. By around 2600 BCE, wood was being used for larger boats.

14

Cutting edge

The Suez Canal in Egypt links the Mediterranean and the Red Sea, cutting thousands of kilometres off the sea route between Europe and Africa. It was finished in 1869, but the Egyptians had been building canals long before that. Under Senusret III (around 1850 BCE), and later pharaohs, a much earlier canal was dug between the Nile and the Red Sea.

Sailing ships

Early Egyptian boats were pushed along with poles or oars but, by about 3200 BCE, the Egyptians had begun to use large, rectangular sails. Sails made travelling up the Nile much easier. Although the Nile flows from south to north, the wind usually blows the opposite way. Boats travelling down the Nile could drift with the current. Sails meant that boats travelling up the river could now use the power of the wind.

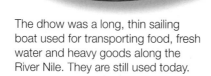

The dhow was a long, thin sailing boat used for transporting food, fresh water and heavy goods along the River Nile. They are still used today.

Boats to heaven

Many small wooden boats have been found in Egyptian tombs, but a truly remarkable discovery was made in 1954. Buried in a pit next to the Great Pyramid of Giza, archaeologists found this almost perfectly preserved, full-sized wooden ship. It had been built for pharaoh Khufu around 4,500 years ago, possibly as a funeral barge to carry his body along the river to his tomb.

Khufu's boat measures around 43 metres long and was made c.2566 BCE. It is built from planks of cedar wood. The boat was found broken into 1,224 pieces, which were painstakingly put together again.

15

Around the world

c.3200 BCE Sumeria
The Sumerians use square-rigged sailing boats to establish trade routes with places as far away as the Indus Valley. They also make river boats from reeds and animal skins.

c.2500 BCE India
The oldest known tidal dock is built at the Indus Valley city of Lothal on the west coast of India. It remains an important centre for the bead trade until around 1900 BCE.

c.1175 BCE Egypt
The Sea Peoples from the Mediterranean are defeated by a fleet of Egyptian warships at the Battle of the Delta, under the command of Pharaoh Ramesses III.

SEEING THE DOCTOR

For their time, the ancient Egyptians had a very advanced system of medicine. Several papyrus documents have been found which describe how to treat injuries and illnesses, showing that doctors understood a lot about how the body worked. Doctors may have been trained by other doctors in their family, although there were probably also medical schools.

16

Cutting edge
The multi-talented Egyptian official, Imhotep (c.2686–2613 BCE), served under King Djoser as chancellor and high priest. A poet, architect and philosopher, he was also one of the world's first known doctors. After his death, he was worshipped as a god. Later he was linked to Asclepius, the Greek god of medicine.

An engraving on stone of the sort of instruments that ancient Egyptian doctors used.

Doctor's kit
Doctors were trained to examine patients, ask questions and make notes about what they found. Treatments included honey, and many different plants and herbs. Some doctors performed simple operations, using surgical instruments. They cleaned and stitched wounds, and amputated limbs — all without anaesthetic for the patient.

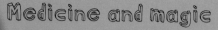

Medicine and magic

Medicine, magic and religion mingled together in ancient Egypt. Many doctors were also priests, and used prayers and magic spells as part of their treatment. Sometimes, sick people spent a night in the temple, hoping to be cured. Several Egyptian gods were linked to medicine and healing. Sekhmet, the lion-headed goddess, was goddess of doctors, and was believed to be able to cure disease and ward off the plague.

A statue of Sekhmet, the lion-headed goddess of doctors. She was also said to protect the pharaohs and lead them in war.

17

Around the World

1792–1750 BCE Babylon
Part of King Hammurabi's 'Code' sets out laws about medicine, such as how physicians should be rewarded or punished, according to the success of their treatments.

c.1500 BCE Egypt
The Edwin Smith Papyrus is one of the world's oldest medical texts. It describes 48 cases of patients with a variety of injuries and wounds.

1600–1460 BCE China
The Shang believe that illnesses are caused by angry ancestors. Oracle bones (carvings on animal bones) show references to headaches, eye problems and stomach pains.

BADGES OF HONOUR

The early Egyptian army was made up of the pharaoh's bodyguard and a small number of professional soldiers. Ordinary farmers and craftsmen were called up in an emergency. In the 16th century BCE, the Hyksos people attacked Egypt. This led to the army being reorganised into a powerful fighting force, led by the pharaoh himself.

This scene, painted c.1340 BCE, shows King Tutankhamun riding a chariot into battle. In reality, he would have had a charioteer to drive for him.

18

Egyptian army

The army was organised into divisions of 5,000 men (4,000 infantry soldiers and 1,000 charioteers). Each division was named after a god, such as Amun or Re. Soldiers had a variety of weapons, including bows, arrows, spears and shields. Another weapon, the khopesh, was a sword with a sickle-shaped blade.

Queen Ahhotep's flies of valour, made in c.1550 BCE. It was very unusual for women in ancient Egypt to be rewarded in this way.

19

Cutting edge

Around the time of the Hyksos invasion, horses and chariots were introduced into Egypt for the first time. Made from wood, chariots were pulled by two horses and manned by two soldiers, armed with bows and arrows. They were speedy and mobile for attacking the enemy, and quickly became deadly weapons.

Flies of valour

Soldiers who showed great bravery in battle were rewarded with land, slaves and jewels, including small golden flies, called 'flies of valour'. A necklace of three golden flies was found in the tomb of Ahhotep I (c.1550 BCE) in Thebes. The flies were given to her by Ahmose I, her son, in recognition of her role in defending Thebes from attack while he was away from home.

 Around the world

c.2600 BCE Sumeria
A mosaic panel, on the Standard of Ur, shows some of the first images of war chariots. They have solid wheels and are pulled by oxen or wild donkeys.

c.1274 BCE Egypt
The Battle of Kadesh is fought between the Egyptians and the Hittites. With perhaps 5,000 chariots taking part, this may be the largest chariot battle ever.

c.1200 BCE China
Chariots appear during the Shang Dynasty but are mainly used for transport and hunting. Several have been found in royal tombs, with horses and charioteers.

DECIPHERING WRITING

20

In around 3200 BCE, the ancient Egyptians became one of the first civilisations to invent a system of writing. It used picture symbols, called hieroglyphs, to stand for objects or sounds. For the Egyptians, writing was sacred. They believed that it had been given to them by Thoth, the god of wisdom.

Scribes at work

Hieroglyphs were very complicated to use. Professional writers, called scribes, trained for many years to read and write them. Good scribes worked in the government, temples or law courts. Some travelled with the army, writing battle reports. Because their skills were so valuable, many scribes rose to positions of power.

A tomb model of a scribe, writing on a roll of papyrus. Scribes wrote with ink and brushes.

Solving the stone

After the Roman conquest of Egypt around 2,000 years ago, the skill of reading hieroglyphs was lost. Then, in 1799, a soldier in Napoleon Bonaparte's army discovered this large stone slab. Known as the Rosetta Stone, it was covered in writing. The same piece of text appeared in three different scripts — hieroglyphs, demotic (a simple Egyptian script) and ancient Greek. By matching royal names in all three, French scholar, Jean-François Champollion, was able to crack the code and decipher the mystery of hieroglyphs.

The Rosetta Stone was originally set up in a temple as a thank you to the Greek ruler of Egypt, Ptolemy V, in the 2nd century BCE.

Cutting edge

Before paper was invented, people wrote on wet clay, stone, wood, metal and bone. The first paper-like material was papyrus, made in Egypt from reeds that grew along the River Nile. Sheets were made from thin strips of papyrus stem, dried in the sun. These were then stuck together to make long rolls for writing on.

21

Around the world

c.4000–3000 BCE Sumeria
Some of the earliest examples of writing are wedge-shaped inscriptions (called cuneiform) on clay tablets from Sumeria. They are temple records.

c.2600–1900 BCE Pakistan/India
Inscriptions from the Indus Valley appear on many carved clay seals but, so far, no one has been able to decipher them or find out if they are a system of writing at all.

c.1200–1050 BCE China
The first evidence of Chinese writing comes from inscriptions on oracle bones from the late Shang Dynasty. The bones were used to communicate with the spirits of the ancestors.

Some of the huge stone pillars in the Hypostyle Hall (c. 1290-1224 BCE) in the Precinct of Amun-Re, Karnak.

TEMPLES TO THE GODS

The ancient Egyptians worshipped hundreds of gods and goddesses. Some were believed to control the forces of nature, such as the Sun and Moon. Others were linked to farming, writing and aspects of daily life. The Egyptians built beautiful temples in honour of the gods, as the gods' homes on Earth. One of the greatest was the temple of Amun-Re at Karnak.

Sacred space

The vast temple complex at Karnak is one of the biggest religious centres ever built. The most famous part is the Precinct of Amun-Re, built in honour of the sun god. This picture (left) shows part of the huge Hypostyle Hall. Its roof (now collapsed) was supported by 134 massive pillars, some more than 20 metres tall. The pillars were carved to look like bundles of papyrus reeds, with the tops shaped like open flowers or buds.

23

Part of a temple frieze (c.1460 BCE) showing the expedition to Punt from the mortuary temple of Queen Hatshepsut at Deir el-Bahari.

Cutting edge

Some pharaohs had temples built where they could be worshipped after their death. These were called mortuary temples. The walls of Queen Hatshepsut's magnificent mortuary temple are carved with scenes of events from her reign (c.1508–1458 BCE). They include the great expedition to Punt to bring back precious myrrh.

Priests and worship

Egyptian temples were private places, reserved for the gods and their priests. The holiest part of the temple was the inner sanctuary, where a statue of the god was kept in a shrine. Every day, the priests dressed the god's statue and offered it food, as if it were alive.

Around the world

1364–1347 BCE Egypt
Akhenaten, previously known as Amenhotep IV, bans the worship of the old Egyptian gods and goddesses and introduces the worship of one god, Aten.

900 BCE India
Religious poems composed by Aryan priests are gathered together to form the *Rig Veda*. It remains one of the most sacred texts of the Hindu religion.

447–438 BCE Greece
The Parthenon is built in Athens and dedicated to the goddess Athena. Its huge size and dazzling white marble are intended to show off the city's power.

EVERLASTING AFTERLIFE

The ancient Egyptians believed that, when you died, your soul travelled to a better life in the next world, but only if your body survived intact. For this reason, they went to great lengths to make sure that dead bodies did not rot away, using a process called mummification.

24

Making mummies

When a person died, embalmers washed the body, and removed the brain and other organs. The body was then packed with a type of salt, called natron, to dry it out. Next it was stuffed with sawdust or cloth, more natron and sweet-smelling herbs, and wrapped in linen bandages. Amulets were placed between the layers and the wrapped body was placed in a coffin.

Cutting edge

The technique of mummification used by the Egyptians worked so well that many bodies have survived to this day. One of the most famous is the mummy of Ramesses II (reigned 1279–1213 BCE) which was discovered in 1881. Today, scientists can examine mummies without having to unwrap them and damage them, using X-rays and CT scans. From these, they can tell what the person died from, and even what food they ate.

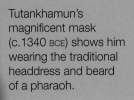

Tutankhamun's magnificent mask (c.1340 BCE) shows him wearing the traditional headdress and beard of a pharaoh.

These jars were used for storing the liver, lungs, stomach and intestines. They were placed in the tomb.

25

Death mask

Sometimes, a mask showing the dead person's features was put over the mummy's head. This was to make it easier for the soul to recognise its body in the afterlife. The masks were usually made from cartonnage – linen stiffened with plaster. Royal masks, such as Tutankhamun's, were made from gold and semi-precious stones.

Around the world

c.5000–3000 BCE South America
The oldest mummies known come from the Chinchorro culture in northern Chile and southern Peru. Around 280 mummified men, women and children have been found.

1600–1460 BCE China
Many bronze pots, jars and cups are buried with their owners for making offerings of food and drink to the ancestors in the afterlife.

c.375–210 BCE Denmark
The body of Tollund man is thrown into a peat bog in Denmark. When it was discovered in 1950 it was so well preserved that some people thought it might be a recent corpse.

TOMBS FIT FOR A KING

Some of the greatest buildings of ancient Egypt are the tombs of the pharaohs. The most famous are the pyramids which were built to protect the bodies of the pharaohs, sealed in a burial chamber, hidden deep inside. Their sloping sides are said to represent the sun's rays, up which the pharaoh's soul could climb to reach the sun god.

26

Cutting edge
The Egyptians had no trucks, cranes or other machinery to help them. This made moving the massive stones incredibly difficult. In the quarry, workers cut the stones with simple chisels and saws, then dragged them to the building site by sledge or barge. The blocks were raised into place, using wooden levers and ramps of rubble and earth.

The Great Pyramid at Giza (c.2566 BCE) still stands in the Egyptian desert today.

Great Pyramid

Standing at around 140 metres, the Great Pyramid at Giza was built for Khufu in about 2566 BCE. For more than 3,800 years, it was the tallest structure in the world. This mighty monument contains more than 2 million blocks of limestone, weighing from 2.5 to 15 tonnes each, and took more than 20 years to build. It was originally covered in polished, white 'casing stones' but these have been mostly stripped away or stolen.

Ruins of the tomb-builders' village at Deir el-Medinah.

Tomb-builders' village

From around 1550 BCE, most pharaohs were buried in the Valley of the Kings, in tombs cut deep into the rocks to protect them from robbers. A village was specially built for the workforce of tomb-builders at nearby Deir el-Medinah. Thousands of letters, bills, prayers and charms have been found, written on scraps of papyrus and pottery. These give us valuable information about the villagers' daily lives and work.

27

Around the world

c.2600 BCE Egypt
The first Egyptian stepped pyramid is built by King Djoser and his architect, Imhotep, at Saqqara. It stands 62 metres tall and is covered in white limestone.

c.2100 BCE Sumeria
The Sumerian king, Ur-Nammu, builds a great ziggurat (stepped temple) to the moon god at Ur. It is 64 metres long and over 30 metres high.

c.390 BCE Mexico
The Great Pyramid at La Venta is built by the Olmecs. It is made from clay and earth, stands 34 metres high and may have been a tomb or acted as a sacred mountain.

SCULPTURE ON A GRAND SCALE

Ancient Egyptian craftsmen turned blocks of stone into spectacular works of art. The best sculptors made grand statues of the pharaohs and gods for temples and tombs. They also made much smaller statues of people, animals, houses and boats that were placed in tombs.

28

Great Sphinx

The huge stone statue of the Great Sphinx guards Khufu's pyramid at Giza. It has the body of a lion and the head of a man, believed to be the pharaoh. The Sphinx was carved from an outcrop of limestone, and is one of the largest and oldest sculptures in the world. Rows of smaller sphinxes often lined the entrances to temples.

The Great Sphinx at Giza (c. 3000 BCE) – one of the most famous ancient Egyptian sculptures.

Cutting edge

Reliefs were made by cutting designs into the surface of the wall, or cutting around the outside of a design, leaving it slightly raised. The scene was sketched on the wall, before the sculptors began carving. Afterwards, the reliefs were painted in colour.

Tomb paintings

The walls of Egyptian tombs were brightly decorated with reliefs (see panel) and paintings. These showed scenes of the gods, battles and daily life, and were not simply for decoration but to help the dead person's soul on its journey to the afterlife. Artists worked in teams, using paints made from minerals, such as copper (green) and iron oxide (red). These were ground into powder, then mixed with water.

29

This tomb painting shows farm workers picking grapes for making into wine.

 ## Around the world

c.3000–1500 BCE Pakistan/India
A seated male soapstone sculpture from the Indus Valley city of Mohenjo-Daro shows a man with a beard, headband and robe. He may be a priest or a ruler.

c.2600 BCE Sumeria
The Copper Bull sculpture is produced in Ur, Sumeria. It is made from wood, covered in copper, and may have come from a temple dedicated to the goddess, Ninhursag.

c.1264 BCE Egypt
Ramesses II builds the great temple of Abu Simbel in Nubia. In front of the temple are four huge statues of the pharaoh, carved out of the rock face.

GLOSSARY

Amputated When a person's limb (arm or leg) or part of a limb is removed.

Amulet Small figure of a god or goddess, or sacred object, worn as a good luck charm or for protection against evil.

Archaeologist Person who studies human history by excavating ancient ruins and remains, such as cities, tombs and artefacts.

Astronomer A scientist who studies the stars, planets and the universe.

Chancellor Head of a country's government or a high-ranking official.

CT scan Way of looking inside the body using X-rays and a computer.

Dynasty Ruling family where power is passed down from one member to another.

Embalmer Person who treats a dead body with oils and ointments to stop it rotting away.

Faience Type of glazed clay or earthenware, made by heating powdered quartz (a mineral).

Infantry Soldiers who fight on foot.

Irrigation System of canals, ditches and pipes used by farmers to bring water to their fields so that their crops can grow.

Loom A machine that weaves threads into cloth.

Mortuary Linked to death or burial.

Myrrh Sweet-smelling gum from trees or bushes that live in Africa and South Asia.

Ochre Natural yellow, red or orange colouring found in rocks and clay.

Pectoral Type of Egyptian jewellery worn as a necklace.

Sanctuary The innermost, most sacred part of a temple.

Scale Set of marks, at regular intervals, used in measurement.

Square-rigged A boat that has square sails.

Winnowing When farmers separate grain from chaff (the dry, scaling casings around the grain). The chaff can then be fed to animals.

30

WEBSITES

http://www.ancientegypt.co.uk/
British Museum website that gives information about Ancient Egypt from gods and goddesses to temples and pyramids, with stories and challenges.

http://www.bbc.co.uk/history/ancient/egyptians/
Find out more about the Ancient Egyptians on this BBC website and play a game where you are an embalmer, preparing a body for burial.

http://video.nationalgeographic.com/video/places/countries-places/egypt/tombs-of-ancient-egypt/
Watch this video to find out more about the world of the Ancient Egyptians, and visit some of their magnificent tombs.

Note to parents and teachers
Every effort has been made by the Publishers to ensure that the web sites in this book are suitable for children, that they are of the highest educational value, and that they contain no inappropriate or offensive material. However, because of the nature of the Internet, it is impossible to guarantee that the contents of these sites will not be altered. We strongly advise that Internet access is supervised by a responsible adult.

TIMELINE

c 3100 BCE Pharaoh Menes unites Upper and Lower Egypt and establishes the first Egyptian dynasty, known as Dynasty I.

c 2686-2181 BCE The Old Kingdom. A time of expansion and learning; also the great age of pyramid building.

c 2589-2566 BCE Reign of Pharaoh Khufu. The Great Pyramid at Giza is built as his tomb.

c 2246-2150 BCE Reign of Pharaoh Pepi II. He rules for 94 years, the longest reign in history.

c 2040-1640 BCE The Middle Kingdom. Pharaoh Mentuhotep makes his capital at Thebes.

c 1290-1224 BCE Reign of Pharaoh Ramesses II. He is famous for building many great temples, including Abu Simbel.

c 1552-1085 BCE The New Kingdom. Egypt builds a huge empire and the greatest power in the Middle East.

c 1347-1337 BCE Reign of Pharaoh Tutankhamun. He is buried in a tomb in the Valley of the Kings.

c 1085-664 BCE Royal power begins to decline and the Egyptian empire breaks apart.

c 525-404 BCE The Persians invade Egypt and rule as Dynasty 27.

332 BCE Alexander the Great takes control of Egypt and founds the great city of Alexandria, which becomes a centre of learning.

323-30 BCE After Alexander's death, Egypt is ruled by the Ptolemaic Dynasty, founded by Ptolemy, a general in Alexander's army.

30 BCE Queen Cleopatra, the last of the Ptolemies, is defeated by the Romans. Egypt becomes part of the Roman Empire.

INDEX

32